Close to the Wind

A play

Richard Everett

Samuel French — London
New York - Toronto - Hollywood

ISBN 0 573 11082 4

Please see page iv for further copyright information

CLOSE TO THE WIND

First produced at The Theatre Royal, Windsor, with the following cast:

Gerry	Keith Barron
Kate	Angela Thorne
Louise	Francine Morgan
Julian	Christopher Villiers
Mary	Faith Brook
Roy	Raymond Francis

Directed by Mark Piper
Designed by John Page
Lighting by Stuart Schofield

The play was subsequently revised and produced at The Mill at Sonning in 1993 with the following cast:

Gerry	Mark Kingston
Kate	Carole Nimmons
Louise	Rebecca Egan
Julian	Christopher James
Mary	Heather Chasen
Roy	Eric Dodson

Directed by Myra Frances
Designed by Michael Pavelka
Lighting by Roslyn Nash

CHARACTERS

Gerry, a middle-aged man
Kate, Gerry's wife
Louise, their daughter
Julian, Louise's boyfriend
Mary, Gerry's mother
Roy, a friend of Mary's

The action of the play takes place in the home of Gerry and Kate, a period house in the Home Counties

Time: a night in winter

ACT I

The living room of an oak-beamed seventeenth century house. It is a winter night

We are seeing the room through the fireplace wall. It is tastefully furnished in a homely cottage style and elegantly finished off, with antique ornaments etc. The room is quite spacious with an alcove housing a small dining table. Upstage c are windows looking onto the garden. To one side is a doorway leading to an unseen kitchen. On the other side is another doorway leading to the hall and stairs, of which we see only a part. There are two sizeable cupboard doors: one by the kitchen door, leading to a cleaning cupboard; the other near the hall doorway, leading to an all-purpose junk cupboard. There are several table lamps which can be switched off individually or collectively from a master dimmer-switch by the hall door. There are also wall lights controllable by a wall-switch. There is a large sofa—perhaps winged, and at least one armchair

The curtains are drawn and the room is dimly lit by one small table lamp

In the half-light, a young girl, Louise, stands and looks adoringly into the eyes of a young man, Julian

Louise I love you.
Julian I love you too... I'm also rather knackered.
Louise Then I'll revive you... (*She runs her hands under his clothing and explores his skin*) Arms up.
Julian What?
Louise Quickly.

She lifts his arms for him and pulls his sweater over his head

Julian Look Lou, would you mind terribly if——
Louise Buttons.
Julian What?

Louise I hate all these buttons.

Julian Exeter is nearly two hundred miles from here, you know.

Louise (*unbuttoning his shirt*) Why do they put them so close together?

Julian I really have travelled quite a long way to see you today.

She slides off his shirt

Louise And now I want you to go even further.

She caresses his torso and at the same time steers him upstage of the sofa

Julian Louise... Just a minute... Look, I'm somewhat done in by the
    journey and——

She stops and stares at him

  What is it? What's the matter?

Louise Julian. I don't know how many times in your life a woman has
    taken advantage of you but it's not something I do very often.

Julian No, I know that.

Louise Then, would you mind just shutting up and letting me get on
    with it?

Julian Right. Sorry.

Louise I can't undo this buckle.

Julian There's a knack. You have to tug it and pull.

Louise You bloody tug it and pull.

He does so. The belt loosens

  Thank you.

*She kisses him swiftly and hard on the mouth and then pushes him
backwards. He disappears behind the sofa. She follows him. A few seconds
pass, then their voices are heard from behind the sofa*

Julian Louise... Ow! Sorry, but can I just ask something?

Louise What?

During the following, items of clothing are thrown over the back of the sofa

Julian Why don't we move somewhere more comfortable?
Louise What do you mean?
Julian The sofa. Why don't we move on to the sofa?
Louise I prefer the floor.
Julian You get splinters on the floor.
Louise Let me worry about the splinters.
Julian What about your parents?
Louise I shouldn't think they've ever done it on the floor.
Julian No—where are they? Supposing they come back.
Louise They've gone to the theatre. We've got the place to ourselves. For
   God's sake stop asking questions and——

*The shadowy half-light is pierced for a moment as car headlights sweep
across the closed curtains. Louise's and Julian's heads pop up from
behind the sofa*

Julian What is it?
Louise I'm not sure.

They watch and listen. Two car doors slam

   Quick! It's them!
Julian Who?
Louise My parents! Who do you think!?
Julian Oh my God. (*He runs around the room in his boxer shorts*) What
   shall I do? Where shall I go?

Louise emerges in her bra and pants, clutching odd bits of clothing

Louise In the kitchen! Quickly!
Julian Where is it?
Louise Through that door.

Julian goes through a door and slams it shut

Louise gathers up more clothing

   Julian enters

Julian It's a cupboard, Louise! It's a bloody cupboard!

The sound of the front door slamming

Louise Never mind.

Louise pushes Julian back into the cupboard. With her arms now full of clothes, she scans the room. She hurries across to the light switch by the door and awkwardly flicks on the lights. She notices Julian's shirt protruding from under the sofa. Unable to pick it up, she opts for pushing it out of sight with her foot. Muffled voices are heard in the hall. Still clutching the clothes, she disappears into the other cupboard

Gerry, aged about fifty, and Kate, in her mid to late forties, enter from the hall. They wander slowly into the room, stop some distance apart and stare vacantly at the room

Kate Well, there we are. These things happen.

Gerry Not to anyone else, they don't.

Kate Stop being such a martyr. Brrr! It's cold. That wind goes right through you.

Gerry I really wanted to see that play, Kate.

Kate We'll go another time.

Gerry Three months in advance I had to book those tickets.

Kate We'll go another time, Gerry.

Gerry I wanted to go tonight. I've been looking forward to it for weeks.

Kate Then re-book and you can have all those weeks of looking forward to it again.

Gerry It'll be off by then.

Kate When?

Gerry Whenever I book.

Kate I thought it was selling out.

Gerry It is.

Kate Then it won't come off, will it?

Gerry They'll change the cast.

Kate Oh, for goodness sake.

Gerry (*calling*) Louise!

Kate She's not here.

Gerry Why are all the lights on?

Kate That was me. It keeps the burglars away.

Gerry What burglars?

Kate They've done two other houses up the road.

Gerry So, what are you trying to do—encourage them? It's like a Harrods window. May as well price everything and be done with it.

Kate The curtains are drawn. They can't see in.

Gerry Then what's the point in leaving the lights on?

Kate Gerry, will you please stop now? You haven't drawn breath since we left the theatre. D'you want a drink?

Gerry No. What a waste of a bloody evening.

Kate Why don't we ring Janine's and have a nice quiet meal?

Gerry I don't want to ring Janine's and have a nice quiet meal.

Kate They do that lovely steak *au poivre*—you enjoyed that last time.

Gerry It'll take more than a steak *au poivre* to redeem this evening.

Kate Come on. It's not too late.

Gerry It is too late.

Kate It's quarter to nine.

Gerry I'm beyond hunger.

Kate Well, I'm going to ring them.

Gerry Jolly good. You do that.

Kate What's their number?

Gerry No idea.

Kate Then I'll look it up, shall I?

Gerry You could try.

Kate (*thumbing through the directory*) Honestly. The slightest disappointment and you stamp your foot and sulk.

Gerry (*sulking*) I'm not sulking.

Kate I don't know what gets into you sometimes.

Gerry My mother, Kate—that's what gets into me. Whenever we include her, she hijacks the outing.

Kate Stop it.

Gerry Who needs terrorists with her on the loose?

Kate It was a misunderstanding—just leave it at that.

Gerry Ridiculous. I'm managing director of a company that'll insure anything down to the Pope's knees—and I can't get protection against my own mother.

Kate Try drafting a new policy. You'd make a fortune.

Gerry No-one would touch it—she's an *act of God*. I book the tickets, arrange the transport; all she has to do is stick her bum in the seat and watch the bloody play.

Kate I'm sure that's what she's doing at this very moment.

Gerry Lucky her.

Kate Does Janine have one "n" or two?

Gerry No idea. Look in the directory.

Kate grimaces—she is *looking in the directory*

Fancy turning up with an extra person.

Kate She didn't know, Gerry.

Gerry Without any warning.

Kate She thought she could get an extra ticket.

Gerry Just like that?

Kate It's a perfectly reasonable assumption.

Gerry She's your mother-in-law. It's breaking with tradition to side with her.

Kate I'm not siding with anyone.

Gerry Yes you are.

Kate She's lonely.

Gerry She's stupid. Sent my father to an early grave—probably see me out as well.

Kate That's an awful thing to say.

Gerry You can't put a foot wrong in her eyes.

Kate Rubbish.

Gerry It's true. She thinks you're wonderful.

Kate She doesn't.

Gerry She does. She shares her wine gums with you.

Kate Only the green ones. And she'd share them with you if you spent more time with her. I can't see this number anywhere.

Gerry (*calling*) Louise. Where is that girl?

Kate Out. I told you.

Gerry Where?

Kate I don't know. Meeting someone.

Gerry Who?

Kate I don't know.

Gerry Well—a man, a woman, a boyfriend—what?

Kate I don't know, Gerry! She didn't say! I'll have to try *Yellow Pages*.

Gerry Who is this man? I want to know what he's like.

Kate I don't even know if it is a man. She's perfectly able to look after herself.

Gerry Is she?

Kate She's managed for three years at Exeter.

Gerry Yes. And doing what, I ask myself.

Kate What most young people do at university.

Gerry Exactly.

Kate Studying, Gerry. You know Louise—she's far more interested in dissecting rats.

Gerry Wasting her time. Before anyone says "knife", she'll have found some bloke and be married. What possible use will a degree in zoology be to her, then?

Kate Oh, I don't know. One false move and she'll have his innards on the kitchen table. Removals. Rest Homes. Restaurants. Right. (*She runs her finger down the* Yellow Pages *columns*)

Gerry slumps in a heap on the sofa

Gerry God, what a shambles! What a complete and utter shambles!

Kate Janine's... Janine's...

Gerry If I buy three tickets, what's the point in her rolling up with a fourth? Especially him—silly old fart.

Kate He and a few other silly old farts fought the Battle of Britain for us.

Gerry Doesn't entitle him to nick my theatre tickets.

Kate He's a Wing Commander. You should show him more respect.

Gerry I do.

Kate You don't. And calling him "Winky" doesn't help. (*She finds the number*) Here we are.

Gerry Why does he keep hanging around my mother, anyway? Hasn't he got a home to go to?

Kate They play bridge together.

Gerry Then he should stick to cards and stop turning up like a hijacker's apprentice.

Kate For the last time: it was a mistake!

Gerry Mistake, my arse. She planned the whole thing.

Kate (*starting to dial*) Don't be ridiculous.

Gerry She had that wild scheming glint in her eye. I've seen it before. She had the same look when she switched hymns at our wedding.

Kate Gerry, I'm going to lose my temper in a minute.

Gerry Oh, she knew all right. She knew that with an extra bod in tow one of us would have to stand down. And if one of us stood down, the other would stand down, too. And with the two of us standing down, she'd have us both out of the way, the evening to herself and a spare ticket to flog at a profit to some poor sucker queuing for returns.

Kate Look! I've told you a hundred times—I was perfectly happy to leave you there and take a cab home. But no—you insisted. You haven't stopped since we got in the car and you're making a terrible meal of the whole thing. A terrible, ghastly, putrid meal! (*Suddenly into the phone*) I'm so sorry. It's Mrs Campbell here. I'd like to book a table for two, please.

Gerry Well, it makes me want to spit. It really makes we want to——

Kate Shut up! (*Into the phone*) Yes, the name is Spittle—sorry, Campbell. Mrs Campbell.

Gerry And as for all that carry-on in the foyer...

Kate (*into the phone*) No, Campbell! Not Mrs Camel.

Gerry All those people pushing and shoving and us in the middle with mother doing *One Potato, Two Potato* to see who stays.

Kate (*into the phone*) Yes, I'm sure we could manage that. Thank you very much. (*She hangs up*)

Gerry It was fixed, Kate—I tell you.

Kate What was fixed?

Gerry When it came to my turn, she did one potato on this hand and two potatoes on that!

She looks at him disdainfully. He turns away, switches on the TV set and stares at it. A depressing documentary drones on interminably. Kate struggles to contain herself

Kate Gerry?

Gerry (*without looking up*) Mmmh?

Kate Do you want to go to Janine's or not?

Gerry Not particularly.

Kate Well, it's too late. They're expecting us.

Gerry Oh, good. Got a table, have they?

Kate In the window where we like it.

Gerry Oh, good. Steak *au poivre* on the menu, is it?

Kate I didn't ask, but I'm sure it is.

Gerry Oh, good. No extra people planning to join us?

Kate A table for two if we leave now.

Gerry Splendid. Isn't this turning out well? I wonder where the catch is— perhaps Michael Aspel will leap from the gents clutching a red book. (*He continues to stare at the TV*)

Kate Shall we go?

Gerry This minute?

Kate Yes.

Gerry What's the rush?
Kate There isn't.
Gerry Good. (*He does not move*)
Kate They've got another booking, Gerry. They'd like us out in sixty minutes.

He turns towards her and suddenly leaps into action

Gerry Right! Terrific! Grab the Rennies and let's go!

In one movement, Gerry grabs his overcoat, switches out the lights and exits

Kate is now in virtual darkness, lit only by the flickering TV set. We hear:

TV Interviewer So would you say you were happy?
TV Woman Oh yes. Deep down we love each other, really.
TV Interviewer as narrator Three months later Janet and John were divorced.

She calmly switches the TV off, the lights back on again and defiantly opens the curtains revealing a snowy night, the garden beyond, and Gerry squashing his face on the window

Kate Aaah! Gerry, don't do that!
Gerry (*through the glass*) The engine's warm, the lights are green and the wind's behind us all the way! Coming?
Kate Yes, I'm coming! (*As she goes*) Stupid little man.

She exits

Gerry moves out of sight

The sound of the front door slamming

Pause

The two cupboard doors open. Louise, wearing a large army greatcoat, and Julian, wearing a cleaner's housecoat, come out

Louise Have they gone?
Julian Think so.

The sound of keys in the front door and voices in the hall

Julian and Louise step calmly back into their cupboards

   Gerry and Kate enter

Gerry Where?
Kate There! On the side!
Gerry (*picking up a bunch of keys*) These aren't mine. They're house keys, anyway.
Kate Well, you had them when you came in. You threw off your mac and—(*feeling in her pockets*) Ah.

Gerry opens the cupboard door. Julian cowers within

Gerry I'll get the spare set.
Kate No, it's all right. I've got them.
Gerry Brilliant.
Kate I must have picked them up as I went out.
Gerry (*slamming the cupboard door*) Can we go now?
Kate (*heading off*) Certainly.
Gerry (*holding up a bunch of house keys*) Oi! Don't you want these?
Kate Those aren't mine. Must be Louise's. Silly girl—we'll have to leave the door off the latch for her.
Gerry Oh yes! Why not? (*He draws the curtains shut*) And while we're at it we'll put a sign on the gate: "Burglars' Convention This Way". Come on!

   Gerry snatches the car keys from her and exits switching off the lights and plunging her into darkness again

Kate re-opens the curtains and switches the lights back on. The car horn sounds impatiently

   She hurries out

We hear the front door slam, the car door slam, the car starting up and pulling away

Still in the greatcoat, Louise steps from the cupboard. She carries the bundle of their clothes and dumps them in the armchair as she approaches the other cupboard

Louise Julian?

The cupboard door swings open. Julian cowers, frozen

Julian You said they were going to the theatre, Louise.
Louise Something must have happened. Are you all right?
Julian No. (*He steps from the cupboard and peers inside the housecoat*) I think I've got frost-bite.
Louise Ooh, let's see.
Julian Get off! (*He waves his arms about to get warm*)
Louise You look ridiculous.
Julian So do you. Whose is it, anyway?
Louise My great grandfather's. He wore it in the trenches.
Julian This? I'm surprised he wasn't arrested.
Louise This, stupid. That belongs to Mrs Dibble, our cleaning lady.
Julian God, I'm cold! (*He digs through the pile of clothes and pulls out his trousers*)
Louise What are you doing?
Julian Getting dressed. (*He finds a T-shirt*) Yours, I think. Have you seen my socks anywhere?
Louise Don't you want to pick up where we left off?
Julian Louise, bits of me are dropping off.
Louise I've still got very little on under here, you know.
Julian I can't find my shirt, either. Have you seen it?
Louise (*flashing open the greatcoat at him*) Joooolian! Jay-Jay!
Julian Shirt, shirt—come on, where are you?
Louise Oh, fine. (*She finds her spectacles and puts them on*)
Julian Brilliant! Is this one of those blow-heater things?
Louise Probably.
Julian Where does it switch on? Louise? Where are you going?
Louise To the kitchen. To change.
Julian Turn on the kettle while you're at it.
Louise Sweetheart, if I could turn on the kettle, I'd run off and have its children.

She exits

Julian switches on the blow-heater

Julian I'll thaw out in a minute, Lou! Honestly! (*He picks up the heater and warms his front with it*) Oh! That's better! (*He points it down his trousers*) Oh, wonderful! This is rather exciting, actually. Lou!

Louise sticks her head round the door

Louise My name is Louise. I'm a woman not a toilet. What *are* you doing?
Julian I think I've invented something—a dry Jacuzzi.

Louise exits, unamused

Oh, come on Louise! (*He is searching*) Where the hell is my shirt? Louise! (*He pulls the sweater over the housecoat*) Oh, sod it. (*He heads for the kitchen*) Now, look...

He exits into the kitchen

Louise (*off*) I'm dressing. D'you mind?
Julian (*off*) Louise...
Louise (*off*) Julian! Get out!

He is ejected from the kitchen and the door slams in his face

He leans on the doorway, arms-folded. He gets down on his knees, pants and scratches at the door and then bays like a dog

The door opens and Louise appears

Up yours, dog-breath!

She slams the door shut as she moves back into the kitchen

Julian barges it open and follows her

Julian (*off*) Right. That's it.
Louise (*off*) Give that back!
Julian (*off*) No! Come out here——

Julian re-appears and leads Louise, now dressed in jeans and sweat-shirt, to the sofa

Louise sits and sulks

Louise I hate you. I absolutely hate you.

Julian Look, I'm sorry—OK? High performance sex isn't my forte.

Louise Should've brought your Zimmer frame, shouldn't you? I wanted this weekend to be special, Jay—that's all.

Julian Special.

Louise Yes.

Julian Driven from the station like I was in a getaway car, thrown on the floor, stripped naked and shoved in Mrs Dibble's cooler—it's a promising start.

Pause

Louise Bloody inconvenient, this—I hope you realise that.

Julian What is?

Louise You! (*She points to her brain*) In here! I want to be a vet, Julian.

Julian I know you do.

Louise I have exams to pass.

Julian I know that, too.

Louise Well, how am I supposed to do that with you leaping about in my head?

Julian Lou, I have to tell you—I'm rather confused.

Louise You're confused. I'm extremely confused. And let me tell you, Julian—being confused does not come naturally to me.

Julian Louise... What's this all about? What do you want?

Louise I don't know. I don't know what I want. Yes, I do—I know exactly what I want. But I want you to want it as well because if you don't want it then I don't want it, either.

Julian What?

Louise To get married.

Pause

Julian Sorry?

Louise Speak, Julian. You have all of five seconds to redeem yourself.

Julian chuckles, uncertainly

Julian Shouldn't you be on one knee with a bunch of...

She stares at him coldly

OK, OK. You've got your specs on—that means you're serious. Well...
Um... Why don't we live together?
Louise Live together.
Julian Yes.
Louise Why not? Lots of married couples do.
Julian You know what I'm saying.
Louise My father would freak.
Julian You're over age, there's not a lot he could do.
Louise Apart from cutting off my allowance, no.
Julian Would he?
Louise Wouldn't you? Why should he be keeping a horny old painter in
bog-roll and cornflakes?
Julian Cheaper than a wedding?
Louise Very funny. So, that's what you want, is it? To live together?
Julian People do.
Louise I know. Most of our friends. And look at the mess they're all in.
Julian Emma and Guy are OK.
Louise Oh, Emma and Guy are fine except Guy's knocking off Denise
Freeman.
Julian I thought Denise was living with Rod.
Louise She is. They've bought a place, mortgaged themselves to the
throat and now can't stand the sight of each other. As neither can afford
to buy the other out, they're ever so slightly screwed. Meanwhile, Rod's
got the hots for Elaine Short.
Julian I thought Elaine was pregnant.
Louise She is. But it isn't Gareth's.
Julian Who's Gareth?
Louise The bloke she's shacked up with. Been an item for years.
Julian Whose is it, then—this kid she's having?
Louise Rod's, I gather. Gareth knows, of course, which is why he's trying
to kick her out and get Denise between the sheets.
Julian Grief. Where do they find the time for it all?
Louise God knows. In an age of safe sex, promiscuity's a full-time job.

By the time you've kitted yourselves out, run through the check list and sussed out your partner's bed history, you're completely off the boil.

Julian is deep in thought. Louise goes to him

Grown-ups playing at mummies and daddies, Jay—I don't want that. Commitment. Call me old fashioned but I haven't got time for anything else.

She looks into his eyes. Julian stares back at her

Julian Denise Freeman?
Louise Julian!
Julian Sorry, Sorry. Listen. Um... What about money?
Louise You're an artist—you're supposed to be broke. There's good money in four-legged care—let me worry about the cash.
Julian Supposing you don't qualify.
Louise To be a vet? Then I'll be a Harley Street specialist like all the others. I'll earn enough.
Julian The kept man.
Louise Wouldn't bother you, would it? You'll get a shopping car and a frock allowance. What do you say?
Julian What about love? I know it's only a detail but I haven't actually heard it mentioned.
Louise You know how I feel. What about you?
Julian I feel empty when you're not around, the thought of you with anyone else leaves me psychotic and I've got five unfinished canvases—all of them portrait commissions, all of them women and all of them look exactly like you. How does that sound?
Louise It's a reasonable start.

He leans to kiss her. She stops him

So?
Julian Yes, OK. I accept.
Louise Accept what?
Julian Your proposal.
Louise What proposal? I'm the woman, air-head! It's me that gets to choose!

Julian Right. Sorry. (*He goes down on one knee*) Louise…
Louise Oh, get up.
Julian (*heading for the door to the hall*) Stay there.
Louise Where are you going?

Julian exits and re-enters with a huge pot plant

Julian (*clipped and British*) Louise?
Louise (*joining in*) Why, Julian. You're such a pillock.
Julian I had to come.
Louise Did you?
Julian Yes. You see. Bloody hell this is heavy. (*He puts the plant down*)
    Be mine, be mine!
Louise Yours, yours?
Julian Do me the honour of becoming my wife.
Louise Oh God. So sudden. I need time to think.
Julian Really?
Louise Yes. It's all right, I've thought. (*She runs to the kitchen door*)
Julian Where are you going?
Louise To tell Mummy and Daddy, put on the kettle and bonk you
    senseless on the kitchen floor.
Julian Shall I come?
Louise Oh, do. Please. It would be such fun.

She exits, and he follows her into the kitchen

Louise screams playfully; the giggling subsides as the door shuts

Brief pause

We hear the front door opening and then slamming shut

An elderly couple, Mary and Roy, enter from the hall

Mary Oooh-ooh! Kate? Gerry? Only me! Oh, it's good to get into the
    warm. Come along in, Roy.
Roy Thank you.
Mary Let's see. Where is everyone?
Roy The lights are on.
Mary The door was off the latch, too.

Roy Bit like the *Marie Celeste*.
Mary It's over an hour since they left us at the theatre. You look in the kitchen, I'll try upstairs.

Mary exits calling upstairs

Roy opens the kitchen door and leans in

Roy Hallo, hallo, hallo! Anyone at home?

A cold, dishevelled and half-dressed Louise nips outside, past the windows. She peers through the glass and then signals frantically to Julian who follows her—also frozen and half-naked. Roy steps back into the room, closing the kitchen door. He takes in the surroundings and focuses on a small framed photo on the wall. He gets out his spectacles and bends down to examine it

Mary enters

Mary Completely deserted. Any joy in the kitchen?
Roy (*still peering at the picture*) 'Fraid not. Just a pile of old washing on the floor.
Mary How very peculiar. I distinctly heard Gerry say they'd go straight home. I didn't notice if their car was outside. I'll have another look.
Roy Righto.

She exits into the hall

Roy continues studying the small picture. We hear the front door opening

Mary (*off*) Oooh-ooh! Kate? Gerry? Are you out here?

Louise and Julian scamper past the windows again from the other direction. The front door slams

Mary enters

  Not a dicky bird.
Roy This picture, Mary.
Mary Mmmh?

Roy On the side, here.
Mary (*getting out her specs*) Oh, that. Yes. My late husband during the war.
Roy Really?
Mary He was a PT instructor on trans-Atlantic convoys.
Roy Was he, by Jove?

They both peer at the picture

Mary That's Jack, there.
Roy Where?
Mary There.
Roy This one?
Mary That one. In the vest.
Roy Right. Got him. Looks a fit sort of chap.
Mary He was. Fine figure of a man. Got torpedoed twice.
Roy Dear me.
Mary Went through all that and fell down dead on Hungerford Bridge.
Roy What bad luck.
Mary Anyway, what now? What happens now?
Roy Abort, I'd say.
Mary Oh dear. Nothing's really gone right this evening.
Roy Domestic engineering isn't your strong point.
Mary And what with the play, as well.
Roy Dreary stuff. Young Gerry was well out of it.
Mary All that cursing and blinding. And what about that girl?
Roy Oh, I didn't mind her so much.
Mary But why did she have to take her clothes off like that?
Roy Quite.
Mary What was the point?
Roy Can't imagine.
Mary One might have understood it if she'd had something to show.
Roy Yes. Very disappointing.
Mary What?
Roy The whole evening. Bit of a let down all round, I'd say. Still. Come on, I'll drive you home.
Mary Oh dear. I would so like to have seen them. Such a good opportunity to sort things out, Roy.
Roy We'll leave it for another time.
Mary Five minutes. Come on. Let's make ourselves a cup of something and see if they turn up.

Roy As you wish. He's your son.

Mary You sit down, I'll put the kettle on. Switch on the television, we might get the news. See if anyone's still running the country or total anarchy has finally set in.

As Mary heads for the kitchen door, Louise opens it with a flourish and enters

Louise Granny!

Mary Aaaah!! Wheezy, darling. You gave me the fright of my life. We thought there was no-one here.

Louise We were in the kitchen. (*To Roy*) Hallo, I'm Louise.

Roy Delighted.

Mary I thought you looked in there, Roy.

Roy What? Oh yes, I did.

Louise Yes, we heard someone call but presumed it was a dog.

Mary A dog?

Louise Barking. We should have looked.

Mary We?

Louise Sorry?

Mary You keep saying "we", darling—as though there's someone with you.

Louise There is.

Mary Oh.

Louise Julian.

Mary Well, are we allowed to see him or is he only for private view?

Louise Julian, come and meet my grandmother.

Julian appears in the doorway next to Louise—an awkward squash

Julian Hallo.

Mary How do you do. And this is Wing Commander Cartwright.

They shake hands

Roy Call me Roy. Everyone does.

Mary We were just wondering where the others were.

Louise Gone for a meal. They'll be a while, I expect. I thought you were all going to the theatre.

Mary We were. We did. We left early.

Roy Come along, Mary. Best press on and leave these two to themselves.

Mary You're looking awfully flushed, my poppet. Not sickening for something, are you?

Louise No, no.

Mary Well, out of my way. I'm about to put the kettle on.

Mary bustles into the kitchen

Roy Unstoppable, that one. Five minutes and we'll be off.

Louise Don't worry. How d'you two know each other?

Roy Oh, we play a spot of Bridge, you know. Keep bumping into each other at the pension till. Ha! She's a good sort.

Louise Yes.

Roy What about you, young man. What do you do with yourself—when you're not visiting young maidens?

Julian I paint a bit.

Roy What, decorating? That sort of thing?

Louise Julian's an artist, Wing Commander.

Roy Roy, please. An artist—my word! How are your ears? Still got 'em both, have you? Ha! Van Gogh, you know—lopped one of his off.

Julian So far.

Roy Well done. Hang on to yer ears, that's what I always say. I suppose that explains the skirt.

Julian Sorry? (*He sees the housecoat hanging down from under his sweater*) Oh!

Roy Dashed here straight from work, did you?

Julian No, it's... Um... (*He tucks it in*)

Mary enters

Mary There we are. It had boiled already so it just needs to brew. How are you three getting along?

Roy Young Julian here's a painter, Mary. Did you know that?

Mary Really?

Roy Pictures and so forth.

Mary Splendid. I dabble a bit, myself. (*She rummages in her pocket*) Have you done Wheezy, yet?

Julian Sorry?

Mary Don't you dare do her with her glasses on. Much prettier without. (*She pulls out a small bag of sweets*) Anyway, jolly good. Have a wine gum.

Julian Thank you.

Mary Hold on—there's a green one here somewhere. There. Well, now. Isn't this nice?

Roy Mary, my dear. I've a feeling we're intruding.

Mary Nonsense. It's my son's house. If I can't——

Roy Gooseberries. I'm talking about gooseberries.

Mary Gooseberries? What are you talking about? What's he talking about?

Louise It's all right. Stay and have your tea, at least.

Mary Wheezy, I'm awfully worried about your colour. (*She feels Louise's forehead*) Look at you—all blotchy round the cheeks.

Roy Been too near this one when he's splashing his canvas. Ha!

Mary Too much hard work, if you ask me. Taking a degree in Zoology, Roy.

Roy Is that so?

Mary Right, let's see if that tea's ready.

Mary exits

Roy Four minutes and counting.

Mary (*off*) Wheezy, poppet—is there a cosy somewhere?

Louise I'll get it! Excuse me.

Louise exits

Roy So sorry, old boy.

Julian Really. No problem.

Roy Oh, I know a bit of bill and coo when I see it. Fear not. We'll be gone in a jiff and vacate the sofa. No, they're like motor cars, women—it's such a damn relief when you get 'em going you sometimes forget where you're heading. Ha! And she's first class, that one. You could do a lot worse than young Lilly there.

Julian Louise.

Roy Yes. Keep a firm grip on her, I should.

Mary and Louise enter with a tea tray

Mary Here we are. What are you two boys up to in here?

Roy Waiting—tongues akimbo. Well done. Shall I be mother?

Mary I'll be mother. You shut up.

Louise You live round here, do you, Roy?

Roy Craddock Lane.

Mary He's got the most beautiful garden backing on to the fields.

Roy Bit of a jungle now, though. My wife took charge of all that—God rest her soul.

Louise You should let Gran loose on it. She loves gardening.

Roy Oh, I have. Came at the climbers in close formation—didn't you, Mary?

Mary I pruned them a bit, yes.

Roy Nonsense! Straight out of the sun, she came and dived for the bindweed. Ha! Down in flames it all went. (*He punches his hand*) Zap!

We hear a bleep sound

Julian What was that?

Mary Oh, don't keep doing that, Roy. I keep telling him.

Louise Granny's keys. You're supposed to whistle and it calls back to you—one of those Christmas gimmicks that never worked.

Mary (*producing the keys from her bag*) Mine does. Marvellous. Responds to anything. It even does it if you sing. Listen...

Roy Yes, all right. Put them away, old thing. You'll lose them, otherwise.

Louise I hope he's paying you, Gran—for all that work in the garden.

Mary Oh, yes. It cost him a meal.

Louise Took her out to dinner, did you, Roy?

Roy No, no. She cooked it. On the Aga. Cleaned it from top to bottom and put it through its paces with a steak and kidney pud. Ha! Now, come along Mary—drink up.

Mary I have barely had a sip.

Roy I know, but the snow and so forth. We should be going.

Louise Can I give Mum and Dad a message?

Mary Ha! Not easily. Could she, Roy?

Roy Not really. Well, jolly nice to meet you both and I hope, once Mary's settled, you'll come and see us.

Julian I'm sure we will. And as soon as we've set a date, you'll be the first to know.

Roy Goodbye then, Giles.

Julian Goodbye, Major.

They both set off towards the hall

Mary Just a moment!

Louise Just a moment!

Mary Wheezy, darling. Has something happened that grandmothers ought to be told about?

Julian and Louise exchange a look

Julian No-one should know ahead of your parents.

Louise No, I agree.

Mary Ha-ha! I knew it! That's wonderful news. I didn't think people did it anymore.

Louise What?

Mary Got married. Apart from royalty of course, but they have to, don't they? It goes with the job—or, it used to. Congratulations, angel. And you, Julian.

Julian Thank you.

Mary Hanky, please, Roy.

Louise But listen. Before we get carried away, here—what's all this "settled" business?

Mary Mmmh? Oh, nothing.

Louise Yes it is. Roy said "When you're settled, you're to come and see us".

Roy and Mary exchange a look

Mary Oh, why not? You explain, Roy.

Roy Your grandmother and I have decided to join forces.

Louise Brilliant!

Mary Yes, but the thing is—we wanted to chat to your mother and father and tell them what we'd got in mind.

Louise To get their approval? How sweet.

Mary Hardly, no! I just didn't want them jumping to conclusions.

Louise How d'you mean?

Roy You have to admit—it's a pretty queer thing for an attractive widow to move in with an old buffer like me.

Louise Not if you're married.

Roy What?

Mary Married?

Louise Yes. Isn't that what you mean?

Roy Good grief, no! Ha! Ha!

Mary No! Good heavens! At our age? Far too complicated. No, we just
   thought we'd close ranks against loneliness. Him in his big house, me
   footling about in my flat—mowing the window boxes—all a bit silly.

Roy So, she's coming to footle about at my place.

Mary A friendly face when you walk through the door.

Roy Someone to watch the news with.

Mary Someone to change a plug. That's all.

Louise Well, I think that's excellent.

Mary But the thing is... Well, your mother and father...

Louise We won't breathe a word. Will we, Julian?

Julian My lips are sealed.

Mary Oh darling, I'm so pleased for you. Mind you, it's about time—but
   then the glasses haven't helped, have they? Now listen here, young man.
   You are a very lucky fellow. Got that?

Julian Yes, ma'am.

Mary You take good care of her. She's very special to me.

Julian I will.

Mary That's it. Keep practising. Hanky please, Roy. (*She blows her nose*)
   Well, I don't know about anyone else but I can't possibly go home
   now—far too much excitement.

Roy Tell you what—why don't we organise a celebration?

Mary Oh yes! Surprise Kate and Gerry!

Roy Assuming, of course, that they approve.

Mary Stuff and nonsense! I've given him the once over and in my book
   he'll do. Come on. We'll need champagne, Roy.

Roy The off-licence. Jump to it, Giles.

Mary I know! At home I've got some fluted glasses that we toasted your
   mother and father's wedding with.

She carries the tea tray into the kitchen

(*Off*) You'll have to help me, Wheezy. Drop us off on the way, Roy.

Roy Supposing Gerry and Kate are back before us.

Mary enters

Mary We'll see the car in the drive. Louise can go ahead and prepare
   the way.

Roy And when she says "Now!", we'll enter as Julian's guard of honour!

Mary What fun! Is this all right, Julian? Not going too fast for you, dear?
Julian No, no. I love all this racy stuff.
Louise Whose car, Roy—yours or mine?
Roy Mine's at the ready.
Louise Mine's outside.
Mary Decisions, decisions! Fists up, you two.

Louise and Roy put up their fists. Mary bangs away at speed

Mary Five potato, six potato, seven potato, *more*! Your car, Roy. You win.
Louise You cheated!
Mary I never cheat except at bridge. Come along chauffeur—chocks
away!

Louise begins turning the lights out

Mary and Roy exit hurriedly

As Julian searches for his shirt, Louise kisses him passionately

Julian Stop, stop. I've got to find my shirt.
Louise Leave it. You're fine as you are.
Julian My sock, too. I've only got one.

She kisses him again. Mary and Roy appear at the window

Mary Come along, you two!
Roy Time for that later!

Louise switches out the lights and they exit

We hear: a door slam, voices, car doors slamming, a car pulling away

Pause

*A light goes on in the kitchen, the door opens and Kate is silhouetted in
the doorway*

Kate Hallo?

She steps cautiously into the room and switches on the lights. She looks round, aware that it is not quite as she left it. She pulls the curtains shut. Something catches her eye under the sofa. She pulls out a shirt, examines it curiously and then discards it

Louise? Are you home, darling?

She sets off into the hall and up the stairs

(*Calling*) Louise? I'm back! Are you up here?

As her voice fades we hear a car pulling up, a car door slamming and keys in the front door

Gerry enters with a carrier bag of shopping. He crosses the room towards the kitchen

Gerry Kate? Are you back?

He exits into the kitchen

Kate enters and hears banging about in the kitchen. She looks round nervously and picks up a poker. She stands by the kitchen doorway and waits

The door opens and Gerry enters

Kate?
Kate Aaah! (*She strikes, then freezes—the poker within an inch of Gerry's skull*)
Gerry What the devil d'you think you're doing?
Kate I thought you were an intruder.
Gerry You could have killed me!
Kate You could have raped me!
Gerry Don't be so bloody silly. When did you get back?
Kate A few seconds ago.
Gerry Walked all the way?
Kate Yes, rather refreshing. I cut across the fields and came up the garden.
Gerry Cooled you off, I hope.
Kate It's not me that needs to cool off. Where did you get to?

Gerry Drove around. Did some shopping.

Kate At this time of night?

Gerry God bless the Asians. I bought some food.

Kate What kind of food.

Gerry The kind you cook.

Kate Ha! If you think I'm going to start cooking...

Gerry You don't have to do anything. Go and sit down.

Kate I'm in no mood for games, Gerry. You left me stranded in a restaurant. What did you think you were doing?

Gerry Leaving you in peace to finish your meal.

Kate What meal? Don't be stupid.

Gerry I'd have come back for you.

Kate How was I supposed to know that? You stormed out with the keys, the money—everything. I had just enough to pay for a bowl of soup— and that was all in loose change.

Gerry I'm sorry.

Kate I didn't know where to put myself.

Gerry I said—"I'm sorry"!

Kate Well, it won't do. Just because the steak *au poivre* was off the menu.

Gerry It wasn't just that.

Kate The waiter was only trying to do his job.

Gerry He was a half-wit.

Kate He was nothing of the sort.

Gerry Then why did he take an order for steak *au poivre* when there wasn't any left?

Kate He didn't know! It's a popular dish.

Gerry But he had to wait until we'd started our soup before telling us.

Kate The place was packed! He was busy! That was no reason to bang the table and throw bread at him.

Gerry He should have ducked.

Kate He couldn't duck, he had a tray of profiteroles—which dropped all over the woman in red.

Gerry So what?

Kate Nothing. Except I know her. She plays Bridge with your mother.

Gerry Give 'em something to talk about, won't it?

Kate No, I'm sorry. It's not a joke. This time you've gone too far.

Gerry Oh, come on, Kate. Please? I've bought some food—a bit of an olive branch—let me make it up to you.

Kate What did you buy?

Gerry A few ingredients.

Kate What?

Gerry Steak *au poivre*.

Kate Oh, for...!

Gerry Come on. Come and sit down.

Kate I don't want steak au bloody poivre, Gerry! I just... I just want to
be left on my own.

Gerry Fine. Suit yourself.

Gerry exits into the kitchen

*Kate pours herself a drink. Gerry is heard banging about and singing. The
singing stops*

He enters brandishing a sock

Gerry Is this yours?

Kate No.

Gerry It was under the grill.

Kate Must be one of Louise's.

Gerry Fond of sock-on-toast, is she?

Kate I don't know.

Gerry shrugs and exits into the kitchen

Kate sips her drink and then downs it in one. She pours another

Gerry enters

Gerry How d'you like it—rare? Medium? What?

Kate I've told you—I don't want it.

Gerry I'll do it medium.

Kate This is happening too often, you know.

Gerry Sorry?

Kate And it gets worse every time.

Gerry My cooking? Well, I do my best.

Kate Don't be obtuse. You know what I'm talking about.

Gerry Food inside you—that's what you need.

Kate You can't wave it away with a couple of steaks, Gerry.

Gerry You can't wash it down with a bottle of gin, either.

Kate What's that supposed to mean?

Gerry Nothing. An observation, that's all.

Kate Been marking the bottle, have you?

Gerry No.

Kate I enjoy a drink from time to time. I find it helps. OK?

Gerry Of course. Can I carry on, now?

Kate Do what you like—you always have.

Gerry Kate. We had a row—people do.

Kate This wasn't a row.

Gerry No? What was it, then?

Kate Rows are about something. This wasn't about anything. It was futile, pointless.

Gerry Look, we set off for a nice evening at the theatre, events conspired against us and we took it out on each other.

Kate Correction—you took it out on me.

Gerry Whatever.

Kate Not whatever. That's what you did. You didn't get your own way so you threw a tantrum.

Gerry I've said I'm sorry. Can't you just accept it?

Kate No.

Gerry Why?

Kate Because I'm not your bloody punch bag. It's happened too many times before.

Gerry Can't really win then, can I?

Gerry exits into the kitchen

Kate (*to herself*) It's not a question of winning. Something's not right. (*She calls to Gerry*) We're barely half way, you know!

Gerry's head appears round the door

Gerry Sorry?

Kate To the finishing line. We've got another twenty-five years of this.

Gerry Oh, fine. Let's top ourselves now and be done with it.

Kate Shut up.

Gerry Yes! Pour me a hemlock and let's drink to oblivion!

Pause

Gerry saunters into the room. Kate examines herself in the mirror

Kate I look a sight. An absolute sight. What?

Gerry I didn't say anything?

Kate Why not? I've just said I look a sight. D'you agree?

Gerry No.

Kate Then, say so! Contradict me!

Gerry Oh, come on. We're past those games...

She looks at him

All right—you look terrific. Marvellous, even.

Kate Liar.

Gerry You do.

Kate You're just saying that.

Gerry You look OK, Kate.

Kate OK isn't good enough. I'm getting old.

Gerry Of course you're getting old. We both are. But, for your age, you look OK.

Kate I don't want to look OK for my age, I want to look ten years younger.

Gerry Why? I've got used to you like that.

Kate All women want to look younger.

Gerry So do men, but I don't go around——

Kate No, they don't. One of nature's injustices—men look better as they gather years. Huh. Certain proof the Almighty's male, that is.

Gerry (*joining her at the mirror*) D'you include me in that?

Kate What, the Almighty?

Gerry No, getting better-looking as I age.

Kate Of course. Better than that spotty gangly youth I bumped into at the altar, anyway. You look very distinguished.

Gerry (*taking a close look in the mirror*) Really. (*He turns to face her*) Come on, Kate. Why are you doing this to yourself? What's wrong?

Kate I don't know. Sometimes I think it's you, sometimes I think it's me, other times I think it's just—us. Ever since we got married our lives have been filled with a series of distractions—wedding, first house, money problems, babies, second house, new job, parents dying and so on. Until now, finally, the children are going, our parents have gone...

Gerry Nearly gone.

Kate Be patient—she'll go eventually. And it's just us. No more distractions. Just you and me—opening and shutting curtains and throwing food at each other in restaurants.

Gerry It wasn't aimed at you.

Kate I know, I know. But I do just wonder sometimes—I really do wonder—if it hasn't all been a gigantic mistake.

Gerry Oh, Kate.

Kate I mean it. I'm not being silly. It really worries me. For all the time we've spent together, all the things we've done... I'm not sure if we know each other at all. (*She is about to pour a drink*) You're right. It's becoming a habit. (*She screws the top back on the bottle*) I suppose all I'm saying is—it's not too late to give each other another chance.

Gerry What?

Kate If we want it.

Gerry With someone else, you mean?

Kate We deserve it, Gerry. No-one could accuse us of not trying.

Gerry Is that what you want?

Kate I don't know. I thought *you* might.

Gerry Never entered my head.

Kate Really?

Gerry Honestly.

Kate I suppose it would be easier if one of us was having an affair. You're not having an affair, are you?

Gerry No!

Kate No, I didn't think so—the kind of state you go off to work in... I'm sorry, I didn't mean that unkindly. You look rather vulnerable toddling off with your baggy suit and briefcase—the cares of the world resting on your slightly rounded shoulders.

Gerry Kate...

Kate But, I'm sure that's what people do, you know. They have affairs to make it easier—make the problem more accessible. Oh, there are rows and they throw things but at least the problem has identity. It's false, of course. The truth is—they're bored. Bored with themselves, bored with each other but they can't quite bring themselves to admit it. So they jump into bed with their secretaries.

Gerry Well, I haven't.

Kate Good.

Gerry Apart from anything else it would play havoc with her sciatica. Who are these secretaries, anyway? These athletic women jumping about the place—one hears so much about them, but I've never met one!

Kate But you are bored.

Gerry No, I'm not.

Kate Yes, you are. We both are, admit it. Weekends here are like a monastic retreat. Two days in silent order and if we go to a restaurant we spend the whole time listening to other people's confessions.

Brief pause

Gerry What do you want, Kate?

Kate I'm not sure. Change, perhaps. I don't know.

Gerry What sort of change?

Kate I feel redundant. And if you suggest evening classes, I'll throw something.

Gerry No, no. I wouldn't be that insensitive. But what about that new health club. Lose a few pounds—do you the world of good.

Kate For God's sake, Gerry! Donning a leotard and working out with Jane Fonda is not everyone's answer to mid-life crisis. I'm lonely. I can't find a peg with my name on it. The rest of the world's rushing purposefully by and I'm left standing at the window.

Gerry You sound like me at the office.

Kate Rubbish. You scramble on the eight-twenty-nine and things start happening around you.

Gerry Someone gets seven across and the train gets stuck on a leaf.

Kate At least you're going somewhere.

Gerry So, what do you want to do—get a job?

Kate Doing what?

Gerry Anything. A woman of your abilities…

Kate Yes, yes, I can get a job. Of course I can get a job, but you're missing the point. I'm talking about *us*. It's not a question of finding something to do. Look. I've brought up a family, I've made you a home, I've dined and small-talked your business colleagues—and that's fine. I've enjoyed it. I don't resent it like a lot of women do. But the basis for all that is you and me—two human beings. I don't need a job, Gerry. I need flesh on the bones of those two people.

Gerry Oh, we're all right.

Kate We're a sham.

Gerry How can you say that? You can't write off twenty three years as a sham.

Kate There's nothing there anymore.

Gerry Of course there is.

Kate Where? Show me. I'm damned if I can find it.

Gerry Affection. Is that what you're trying to say? D'you feel I've neglected you?

Kate I don't feel anything. Can't you see? Can't you understand a single word of what I'm saying?

Gerry I'm trying to, Kate, but to be perfectly honest—it's a bit hard to get hold of.

Kate Go and have your steak.

Gerry No.

Kate I'm going to bed.

Gerry You want me to come?

Kate Do what you like.

Gerry Tell you what—go and have a nice long soak and I'll be up shortly with a bottle of wine. Mmmh?

Kate Oh God.

Gerry Kate, I'm reaching out, here!

Kate How very kind of you.

Gerry For crying out loud, woman—what do you want?

Kate I want to know if anyone's there, Gerry. A person. Two people. I want to point to them and say: "There! You see? That's why I did it. That's what it's all for!"

Pause. Gerry looks lost

A reminder, the smallest gesture—something—to tell me that you do still actually care.

Gerry Of course I care. What do you want me to do?

Kate Anything!

Gerry I've just suggested we go up to bed.

Kate Oh, please. Something real. Something—spontaneous. Oh, I don't know.

Brief pause. Gerry starts unbuttoning his shirt

What are you doing?

Gerry What does it look like?

Kate Don't be silly, Gerry. What are you doing?

Gerry (*pulling off his shirt*) Something spontaneous, you said.

Kate Not that, you idiot!

Gerry (*approaching*) Remember the old days?

Kate Please, Gerry! You look ridiculous in your vest! Aah!

He takes her in his arms clumsily and they fall onto the sofa

Ow! My bracelet's caught! (*She is between anger and laughter*) Get off me, Gerry! Please!

The sound of the front door slamming

Louise (*off*) Hiya! I'm back!
Kate Quickly! Quickly! It's Louise!
Gerry Oh my God!

They scramble off the sofa. Gerry heads for the kitchen, Kate throws him a shirt

He catches it and exits

As Louise enters, Kate tries to compose herself

Louise Thought I saw lights on.
Kate Hallo, darling. Had a nice time?
Louise Yes, thanks. Where's Dad?
Kate No idea.

The sound of Gerry banging about in the kitchen and singing

Louise Who's that banging about in the kitchen, then? Mum?

Kate begins to weep silently. Louise holds her

Hey, hey! What is it? What's happened? Dad! Will you come in here a minute, please?
Gerry (*off*) Shan't be long!
Louise *Now!*

The sitting room door bursts open from the hall, as Mary and Roy enter, making a guard of honour with golf clubs and walking sticks. Julian follows, clutching a bottle of champagne and a box of glasses. Mary and Roy sing the wedding march

Mary
Roy } (*together*) Ta-dum-te-dum! Ta-dum-te-dum!

Gerry enters from the kitchen. He is brandishing two raw steaks and a meat hammer, and wearing what has to be Julian's shirt

Black-out

CURTAIN

ACT II

A few seconds later

Everyone is in the same positions as before: Roy and Mary with sticks raised, Gerry clutching the meat hammer and steak, Julian holding the bottle of champagne. They stare off in the direction of the hall. Kate and Louise have evidently just left the room. The champagne cork pops voluntarily

Julian Oh. Dear me. Um...

Mary Quickly someone—glasses!

Gerry It's all right—use this.

Gerry empties dried flowers on the floor and thrusts the vase underneath the bottle

Roy Well done.

Gerry You lot obviously had a good time.

Mary Gerry, dear—is Kate all right?

Gerry Yes, fine.

Mary She looked terribly upset.

Gerry Louise will cope. I must say, it was very sweet of you to do this. Quite unnecessary. We'll have to pass it round like a loving cup.

Mary Oh, no, we won't. You see what I've brought. Where's that box, Roy?

Roy (*passing the box*) Here.

Mary Now then, Gerry. I bet you don't know what these are. (*She lifts a glass carefully out of the box*)

Gerry Um. Glasses?

Mary Silly fool. Of course they're... Oh, Look. My keys. (*She finds them in the box*) That was lucky. Wheezy must have put them there.

Gerry (*taking the keys*) You don't still use this thing, do you? (*He whistles, it bleeps back*) Ha! And it still works.

Mary Never mind that. These glasses, Gerry—where d'you think they came from?

Gerry Filled up the Rover did you, Roy? The Shell garage up the road?

Mary We toasted yours and Kate's health with them at your wedding.
Gerry Oh! Really?
Roy Sentimental old thing, isn't she?
Gerry Absolutely.
Mary Take care of your memories, that's what I always say. No-one else will do it for you.
Gerry Look... Um. What? Why? Why don't we all sit down?
Mary Good idea. Julian's been telling us about his painting, Gerry.
Gerry Has he, indeed! Who's Julian?
Julian I am.
Gerry Oh. Right. Forgive me. How do you do?
Julian Hallo.
Gerry Is that where you met, then. At painting classes?
Julian Sorry?
Gerry Or do you play bridge, as well?
Julian Bridge?
Gerry Yes.
Julian No.
Gerry Oh. How d'you know these two gad-abouts, then?
Mary He doesn't. Hadn't set eyes on him til tonight—had we, Julian?
Gerry I see! Of course! The extra ticket. How was the play, by the way?

Louise enters

Oh, hallo, darling.
Mary Here she is!
Roy The lady herself!
Gerry Everything all right upstairs?
Louise Think so.
Gerry Jolly good. I've just been finding out what everyone's been up to.
Louise Oh... Right.
Gerry This is Julian, by the way. Julian, this is my daughter Louise.

Awkward pause. All except Gerry exchange confused looks

Well, say something one of you. Julian's a painter, darling.

At a loss, Julian offers his hand. Louise is about to shake it, then brushes it aside. Before she can say anything—Gerry is off again

Now then. The play, Mother—you were about to tell me.

Mary What, dear?

Gerry Up to expectations, was it?

Mary Oh, that. No. Frightful.

Gerry What?

Mary Wasn't it, Roy?

Roy Terrible. Well out of it, old man.

Gerry At least you saw it.

Mary Some of it, yes.

Gerry What d'you mean? There weren't pillars in front of you? Not with tickets at that price.

Mary No, no. The seats were fine.

Roy We only saw the first twenty minutes.

Gerry I don't understand. A bomb scare, or something?

Roy No. We walked out.

Pause. Gerry fumes

Gerry You did what?

Mary Couldn't make head nor tail of it.

Roy Didn't know what they were all banging on about.

Gerry Hold on. There's an air of conspiracy about all this—are you pulling my leg?

Mary No. We didn't like what we saw, so we left. It hardly matters...

Gerry Hardly matters?

Louise Dad——

Gerry Just a moment, Louise. After all that carry-on in the foyer about tickets? Three months in advance I had to book those seats.

Roy Mary said. Very bad luck.

Gerry Bad luck? I'd been looking forward to it for weeks! And we gave up our tickets for you.

Mary I know, dear.

Gerry For you, Mother! So that you and Biggles could see the play!

Mary Roy is a Wing Commander, Gerry. I think——

Gerry And you actually walked *out*?

Louise Dad——

Gerry Louise! Will you please stay out of this?

Louise God.

Gerry (*rounding on Julian*) What about you? Were you in on this? What's your name again?

Julian What? Oh. Julian.

Gerry You marched out as well, did you, what-ho Julian?

Louise Dad, Julian didn't see it at all.

Gerry What?

Mary We keep trying to tell you, Gerry—we only met him for the first time tonight.

Gerry I know! I know! Queuing for returns—I'm not stupid! Well, if he didn't even see it, I'll have my money back, Mother. (*To Julian*) What did she charge you for the ticket?

Julian Sorry?

Gerry How much did you pay her?

Julian Nothing. I didn't.

Gerry You mean you got it for free? Oh, that's marvellous, isn't it? Typical of this generation! They get everything handed to them on a plate and—

Louise Dad! *Shut up!*

Kate enters, now in a dressing-gown

Kate What on earth is all this shouting about?

Gerry Ah, hallo, darling. I'm just getting the low-down on the play— apparently our sacrifice was in vain.

Louise Come and sit down, Mum.

Kate It's all right, I'm fine. What's going on, exactly?

Gerry Quite simple. Roy, Mother and Pablo Picasso here didn't think much of our choice of play—so they walked out.

Louise For God's sake, will you listen a minute?

Gerry Isn't that right, Mother? Hallo? Tango base, tango base. Are you receiving me—over?

Mary I think it would be better if Roy and I left.

Gerry Well, what I say is... (*He lifts the vase*) Here's to a thoroughly well-organised cock-up by a bunch of Philistine slobs! Cheers! (*He drinks deeply from the vase*)

Kate Have you quite finished?

Gerry No, there's a drop more for anyone that wants it.

Kate Why don't you go in there and finish whatever it was you were doing?

Gerry Oh, the champagne fizz! It's gone right up my nose!

Kate Please, Gerry—now!

Gerry Right! Wanted yours rare, didn't you? Fine. Medium it is, then. Excuse me.

He exits into the kitchen

Louise and Kate exchange looks

Louise Is that it, d'you reckon? Or does the cabaret have a second half?
Kate I've a feeling it's just begun.
Roy We'll be pushing along, my dear.
Mary Yes, there's obviously been a misunder——

Gerry enters

Gerry Anyone seen a couple of steaks? I had them when I came in.
Louise Oh God.
Kate Roy and Mary are just leaving, Gerry. Would you like to say goodbye?
Gerry Love to. So soon? It's been a joy and pleasure, Wing Commander.
Roy Look, I'm sorry about the play, old boy. Perhaps another time we could...

Gerry frisks Roy up and down

What are you doing?
Gerry Just checking to see if you've got our steaks.
Kate Gerry!
Gerry Sorry, darling. Easy enough to do—you leave someone's house and pocket a couple of steaks as you go. Nope, he's clean. Chocks away, Winky!
Kate I'll see you out.
Mary (*leaving*) Don't come into the cold, dear—not in your dressing-gown.
Kate (*following her*) I'm fine. I'll see you to the door.

They exit

Julian and Louise are alone with Gerry who suddenly sees his steaks

Gerry There they are! (*Kissing the meat*) Mmmh! My little beauties. Oh. Bit of fluff. Never mind. Night, night, Picasso—keep up the good work!

He exits into the kitchen

Julian You've seen what he's wearing, haven't you?
Louise Yes.
Julian How am I going to get it back? It's my favourite shirt.
Louise You could ask.
Julian Oh, very funny. Is it often like this, here?
Louise Depends on the moon. (*She puts her arms round him*) But no-one—has ever escaped—the vampire's daughter!

Louise buries her teeth in Julian's neck

Gerry enters

Gerry I thought you were going.
Louise Julian is a friend of mine.
Gerry So it would appear. Fast worker, eh? Quite a productive evening for you: our theatre tickets, their champagne, and now you're after my daughter.

Kate enters

Kate I hope they get back safely. It's snowing hard and drifting in the wind.
Gerry Oh, Winky'll make it...

Using a tea-towel as a propeller, Gerry zooms towards the kitchen with attendant engine noises

(*He speaks from the door*) Re: the steaks, my angel. They're under the grill as I speak.
Kate For the last time—I don't want it! Perhaps these two are hungry.
Louise Not for me. (*To Julian*) You go ahead, though.
Julian Well... Um...
Gerry Yes! What a good idea! Must have worked up quite an appetite.

He exits

Kate I haven't said hallo, properly. Julian, isn't it? We met the weekend I came down to Exeter on my own.
Julian That's right.
Kate We discussed Matisse on Louise's staircase.
Julian I remember.

Kate So. Passing through, are you?

Julian Sort of.

Kate How nice. Where are you off to?

Julian Um... Nowhere.

Kate Oh.

Louise He's staying put.

Kate Ah.

Louise Here.

Kate Right.

Louise If that's OK.

Kate Of course. I just wish I'd known—I'd have made up a bed for you.

Louise Oh—we can do that.

Kate Fine. Well. It's lovely to see you.

Louise Actually, Mum... Julian's come to see me.

Kate Well, obviously, darling. I may be old, but I'm not stupid. You're most welcome, Julian—stay as long as you like.

Gerry enters. He camps about

Gerry The thing is, Pablo—I'm having mine as steak *au poivre*, but you could have yours just plain, if you want it.

Julian Um. Well. Whatever.

Gerry No, not "Um-well-whatever". How would you like it—*au poivre* or just *garni*?

Julian Um...

Gerry Too late. *Au poivre* it is.

Kate I'm putting Julian in your study, Gerry—is that all right?

Gerry Can't he eat it in here?

Kate To sleep.

Gerry Sleep.

Kate Yes.

Gerry Here.

Kate Yes.

Gerry The whole *night*?

Kate No, the weekend, I expect. Won't you, Julian?

Gerry Dear God—he's unbelievable, this man... (*He bows Poirot-like*) Dinner will be served shortly, *monsieur*.

Kate Gerry?

Gerry Yes, my love, my sweet.

Kate What have you got on?

Gerry What do you mean?

Kate That shirt. I've not seen it before.

Gerry Well, it's odd you should mention it because neither have I.

Kate It's hideous. Take it off immediately.

Gerry Certainly...

He strips off. Louise buries her head in her hands

Better? No? OK, let's try the vest as well.

Kate Gerry! (*She throws his original shirt at him*)

Gerry Excuse me—my cooker calls.

Draping the shirt over his shoulder, he minces back into the kitchen

Louise Is it hereditary, d'you think?

Kate Probably. (*She examines the shirt Gerry has taken off*) Where on earth did he get this?

Julian Well, actually...

Kate It's filthy. Poof! And it smells.

Louise Mum, he thinks Julian's been to the theatre with Gran.

Kate What?

Louise He saw them arrive together. Explain it to him, will you?

Kate Yes, what was all that with her and Roy and sticks at the door. What was going on?

Louise Ah. Well.

Kate And the champagne? What were you all doing?

Louise Well...

Kate I know that look, Louise. What have you been up to?

Louise Why don't you sit down?

Kate What for?

Louise Because when you tell Dad that Julian isn't a friend of Granny's and he didn't walk out of his stupid play, would you also tell him he's his future son-in-law?

Gerry enters triumphantly with two steaks and a tray

Gerry *Dar-ant!*

Kate What did you say?

Gerry I said: "*Dar-ant!*"
Kate Not you. Louise—would you mind repeating that?
Louise Julian?

Julian takes a deep breath

Julian Mr Campbell, I want to marry your daughter.

Brief pause. Then Gerry bursts out laughing

Gerry Now look, old man. I'm sure you're a terribly nice chap and all that. But you can't just step in off the street, stroll in here and start taking our women! All right? So, unless you're looking for a punch in the gob, I suggest you eat your steak and go.
Kate Gerry, will you please be quiet?
Gerry No.
Kate Shut up! Louise?
Louise Aren't you pleased?
Kate Of course. Yes. It's a bit sudden, that's all.
Gerry Oh, I don't know, darling. Half an hour these days and they're usually pregnant.
Kate Gerry! Louise has invited Julian to stay because he's a friend of hers!
Gerry I know that. He's on the rebound from a brief fling with Mother.
Kate From Exeter, Gerry! Julian is from Exeter! (*To Louise*) Darling, of course, I'm pleased. I just need a moment or two to take it in. (*She sits*) Gerry, do say something, for God's sake.
Gerry My steak's getting cold. Anyone mind if I carry on?
Kate Our daughter's getting married. Will you please respond?

Gerry settles himself at the table and forks in a mouthful of steak

Gerry Well... First off—an initial reaction, you understand—I think I'd say—terrific.
Louise Really?
Gerry But I think it could have done with a bit more pepper. Come on Julian—yours is getting cold.
Louise I'm sorry, but I don't need this. Let's just leave it till the morning, shall we?
Gerry How long have you known each other?

Louise Mind your own business.

Gerry Julian?

Julian About six months. I have a small studio in Exeter.

Gerry Come on, man—tuck in! Six months, eh?

Julian About that.

Gerry You've never mentioned this bloke before, Louise.

Louise I have actually—but you don't listen. And he isn't a bloke.

With a mouth full of food, Gerry stares at her and then across at Julian

Gerry Oh dear. What is he, then?

Louise His name is Julian. Kindly don't talk about him as though he wasn't here.

Gerry Sorry. And you get on all right, do you?

Louise We love each other.

Gerry Do you mind? I'm talking to Julian.

Julian I think so.

Gerry You think so. No irritating little habits?

Julian Like what?

Gerry I dunno. Toenails in the bed—that sort of thing?

Louise Oh, please.

Gerry Every night, before she gets into bed, Kate, my wife, snips hers into the waste-paper basket. Drives me potty. Personally, I peel mine under the bedclothes when she's asleep—much more civilised and rather satisfying.

Kate Gerry, I think you should stop this now.

Gerry So, Julian—how are you on the toenails front?

Julian I think we're both intelligent enough to know what we're doing.

Gerry Brave words, my friend. Pass the mustard, will you?

Louise Look, what is it with you two? There's an atmosphere here I could cut with a knife.

Gerry We're not talking about us, we're talking about you. You're still not eating your steak, old man.

Kate Gerry, if Louise would rather we left this until the morning, then so we shall. For my part, I'm sorry I wasn't instantly pleased—I was a bit thrown. I'm quite delighted. Congratulations, darling. (*She kisses her*) And you Julian. (*She kisses him*) I'm sure, come the morning, we can have a proper celebration drink.

Gerry Off to bed, are you?

Kate I've had it, frankly.

Gerry Sleep well.

Kate Louise will show you where everything is, Julian.

Louise watches as Kate makes for the door

Louise No, I'm sorry. There's something going on here and I'd like to
   know what it is.

Gerry Your mother's off to bed. Nothing to be alarmed about—it happens
   from time to time.

Kate Bit of a row, darling—that's all.

Louise What about?

Gerry Nothing! Nothing at all. Was it, Kate?

Kate No. It wasn't about anything.

Louise Well, something's going on. It must have been about——

Gerry Louise, darling—drop it!

Kate Anyway. I'll say good-night.

Louise No, don't. Please wait.

Brief pause

Gerry (*pushing his plate away*) Well, that was quite delicious, I must say.
   Now then, the row between your mother and me has nothing to do with
   the matter in hand. So let's just deal with one thing at a time, shall we?
   You sir, I have never clapped eyes on until tonight, so you must forgive
   me—*a*—for mistaking you for someone you were not and—*b*—for
   treating this whole affair with a degree of scepticism. You accept?

Julian Yes.

Gerry Excellent. Off to a good start. I'm beginning to like this chap
   already. Now, I'll work on the assumption you're an honest sort and, as
   one straight-dealing fellow to another, I'll tell you precisely what I
   think. Firstly, you're a painter—so won't have a penny to your name.

Louise You don't know that.

Gerry Has he?

Louise Ask him.

Gerry Have you?

Julian No.

Gerry Right. But money isn't everything, so I'm not that bothered. What
   does bother me, however, is this little thing here. She's called Louise

and it may surprise you to learn, young Julian, that you have competition. Despite all appearances to the contrary, I too love her very much. Next to my signed photo of Douglas Bader, she's my most treasured possession. So I'd like to make it perfectly clear that if you hurt so much as a hair of her head—I'll see to it you never lift brush to canvas again. Not going too fast for you, am I?

Julian No.

Gerry Good.

Louise Excuse me, Don Corleone——

Gerry No. Just wait. That apart, you seem genuine enough and Louise is a single-minded girl. In my view she could do a lot worse—if she hung on a bit, she might do a great deal better but the clock ticks by and one can't have everything.

Louise Is this a long-winded way of saying you've no objection?

Gerry To what?

Louise I'm going to throw something in a minute.

Gerry I think it's a disastrous idea. Much better if you lived together. (*He picks up the plates*) Finished, dear boy? Dear me—she'll have to do something about your appetite. Excuse me. I'll clear these away.

Gerry exits into the kitchen. Brief pause

Louise What did he just say?

Kate He wants you to live together.

Louise But we don't want... Oh, I give up. I can't keep pace with your generation, at all.

Gerry enters

Gerry The point is, my angel—you don't know each other.

Louise How the hell do you know?

Gerry Six months? Not a chance. Common sense.

Louise Bullshit.

Gerry Fine. Do it, then. But my advice is that you give it more time— avoid the heartache of a painful mistake and set up shop together first. Most people do. So, give it a try, see how it feels and, if it works, go for it. If it doesn't, then you'll both be older and wiser, won't you?

Louise I don't believe I'm hearing this.

Gerry Coffee anyone? No? Just me, then.

He exits

Brief pause

Louise Wonderful, isn't it? Just when you think you've got it right, you get
    shat on from left field. (*To Kate*) There's no pleasing your lot, is there?
Julian Louise?
Louise What?
Julian Why don't I make myself scarce for a——
Louise You stay right where you are. I'm not standing for this.

Louise exits into the kitchen

Kate Ah. Now, if you've a tin hat about your person, Julian—you might
    need it.

*During the following, Julian and Kate listen side by side on the sofa. As
Julian looks increasingly unnerved, Kate reassures him with a smile and
a touch of the hand*

Louise (*off*) You—are a selfish, insensitive slob! All my life I've been
    dogged by your fatuous remarks and negative criticism! You're a
    difficult, pompous and thoroughly objectionable old fart! God help
    Mummy when she gets older, that's all I can say! If she's got any sense,
    she'll do us all a favour and stick two barrels of shotgun up your bum
    when you're not looking!

Louise enters and turns to deliver the final volley through the door

I don't want your advice, I don't care what you think. It's third-rate,
pseudo-liberated horse-shit, anyway! (*To Julian*) Primal stuff. That's
the first time I've yelled at him without bursting into tears. Excuse me.

Louise exits into the hall

*The sound of the front door slamming and then a heartfelt explosion of
crying*

Gerry sticks his head cautiously round the kitchen door

Gerry Is it safe?

Kate Yes. You can come out now.

Gerry What on earth was that?

Kate Your daughter.

Julian Perhaps I should go and find her.

Gerry I'd steer well clear if I were you.

Kate Shut up, Gerry. Go if you want to, Julian—but you might find she's best left.

Gerry What on earth brought that on?

Kate Oh, I can't imagine. Well, I think we've done enough damage between us—shall we go up?

Gerry I can't sleep after all that! I'll have nightmares. I need a drink—what about you?

Kate No, thank you. And bring yours up. Good-night, Julian. I'm sorry... Well... You know.

Julian Look, can I say something before you go?

Gerry Fire away. Everyone else has.

Julian Well... I'm a painter not a poet so you'll have to bear with me. I've listened to what you've said, Mr Campbell, and you're absolutely right. Louise and I know each other hardly at all. As you rightly point out, knowledge of someone is something you gain over a period of time. The voice of experience speaking, no doubt. Well, obviously it was—you've been at it long enough. Ha! Sorry... I didn't mean...

Gerry Press on, you're doing fine.

Julian Louise is a determined person and she's strong on commitment. She knows the risks—we both do. Mistakes in marriage are common-place. But that shouldn't stop us from giving it our best shot, should it?

Gerry Best what, did he say?

Kate Shot.

Julian The point is, living together is a commitment of sorts—but it's no real test. It's like people who have close-to-death experiences. They try to tell you what it's like on the other side and can't. Because they haven't actually done it, have they? Died, I mean. Because if they had, they wouldn't be around to tell you, would they?

Gerry Marriage and death are synonymous. Is that what you're saying?

Julian Yes... No! What I mean is—living together isn't marriage. You can't try it, you can only do it. Grab hold and jump, as it were. A lot of our friends are shacked up together and made a complete porridge of it. They're in limbo, and I've no reason to suppose we'd do any better.

Gerry Go on.

Julian We'd buy a place and put down roots and then have the legal
knitting to make sure we were bound to the property but not to each
other. Then we'd wake up one morning and find we were thirty. "Good
grief!" we'd say, "Thirty already? Let's have babies before it's too
late!" "What?" I'd say, "Sire a bastard? We must marry at once!" So off
we'd toddle to the registry office, make a half-baked commitment and
convince ourselves we'd done it because we wanted to. In point of fact,
we'd have done it for the kid who would carry a sack-load of hidden
resentment on its tiny shoulders because its insistence on being born had
forced its parents into holy wedlock. Twenty years later we'd wake up
again and find we were fifty——

Gerry This should be interesting.

Julian We'd congratulate ourselves on getting that far, wonder who the
hell we were and check the cash reserves for therapy or divorce. The
carnage would be everywhere. Two world wars would have nothing on
us. All of which sounds like a pretty average waste of time to me.

Brief pause. Gerry draws breath to speak. He isn't quick enough

One man, one woman appeals to us more, Mr Campbell. I know it's
eccentric and the neighbours will talk—but there it is, I'm afraid.

Gerry attempts to speak. Again, too late

Let me put it another way. I intend to marry your daughter and it would
mean a great deal to her—and therefore to me—if you showed some
enthusiasm. When Louise returns, would you please do so?

*Gerry, now slightly taken aback, is about to reply, when Kate stifles a
laugh*

Kate Not a word. I didn't say a word.

Gerry Good. Now then, young man——

Kate Congratulations, Julian. You got a word in edgeways—in this house
that's quite an achievement.

Gerry Except at weekends when we're on silent retreat. Anyway, thank
you for that. A wise head on young shoulders—something of a rarity,
these days. However, an even wiser head still sees nothing wrong in——

Julian Oh, there's nothing wrong—of course there isn't. Many feel it's an entirely appropriate arrangement. Well, for goodness sake—there's Louise's granny and the Wing Commander, for a start! Ha!

Pause. Gerry stares at him blankly

Gerry Who?
Kate Roy and Mary?
Julian Yes, joining forces—isn't that what they're planning?
Kate I don't know. Is it?
Julian Um...
Gerry Living together, you mean?

Julian swallows deeply

Kate Julian?
Julian No. I don't know. Forget I said anything. Would you mind terribly if I used your bathroom?
Kate Yes. No. Up the stairs, second on the right.
Julian Thank you. Shan't be long.

Julian exits speedily

Gerry and Kate stare at each other

Kate Ha! What on earth d'you make of that?
Gerry No idea.
Kate Roy and Mary?
Gerry Dear, oh dear. The minds of some people.
Kate It was a very odd thing for him to come out with suddenly.
Gerry He's a very odd young man.
Kate You don't think there's anything in it, then?
Gerry Of course not. He just made it up on the spur of the moment.
Kate What if he didn't?
Gerry Talk sense, Kate—please.
Kate Where would he have got it from?
Gerry The papers, probably. The *Sun*, most likely. They do, you know—these arty types.
Kate There could be something in it, you know.

Gerry There isn't. I've read it. It's all bosoms and gossip.

Kate She's been over there quite a bit, pottering about in his garden.

Gerry Look, he was trying to make a point which backfired, so he withdrew it, all right?

Kate Yes, all right.

Gerry Please. Let's change the subject and talk about something else.

Brief pause

My mother moving in with another man, I ask you. Can you see her doing such a thing? Without even talking to us first?

Kate Perhaps she was going to. Perhaps that was what this evening was all about.

Gerry Kate! He made it up, all right?

Kate Fine, fine. He made it up.

Gerry Just forget it.

Kate (*suppressing a giggle*) I'm trying to.

Gerry D'you want a drink?

Kate No, thank you.

Gerry pours himself one

Gerry Huh... (*Mimicking Julian*) "Louise's granny and the Wing Commander".

Kate I still don't see why——

Gerry Kate, will you please just drop it?

Kate You keep bringing it up.

Gerry I'm dismissing it. Thinking aloud. Throwing it out as absurd.

Kate Fine.

Brief pause

Gerry I mean, for a start she'd kill him.

Kate Perhaps he belongs to Exit.

Gerry This is not funny! I must have a firm word with that boy. It's exactly how rumours start. Before we know it, it'll be all round the village.

Kate What will?

Gerry Mother and Winky swinging from the chandeliers. I won't have it.

Kate You won't have much choice—she's over-age, remember. Anyway, I think it's charming.

Gerry It's grotesque.

Kate Two old people holding hands in the dark?

Gerry Look! This is my mother we're talking about!

Kate Tell me something: why is it all right for Julian and Louise, but not all right for Roy and Mary?

Gerry Louise and Julian are young.

Kate Roy and Mary are old.

Gerry Exactly.

Kate So?

Julian appears in the doorway

Gerry Ah, there you are. Find it OK?

Julian Yes, thank you. No sign of Louise?

Kate Not yet.

Gerry Come and sit yourself down, Julian. Drink? Brandy, whisky?

Julian Nothing. Really. I'm sorry for what I said about Mary and Roy. Will you forget I mentioned it?

Gerry Of course! We were just laughing to ourselves about it. Weren't we, darling? Noting your active imagination... Which we presumed it was.

Julian Yes. Well...

Gerry Yes! Thought so. Cheers. Wouldn't want to start up a rumour, would we?

Julian No.

Gerry Start blurting things out at the wrong moment.

Julian No, no. I'm sure they'll tell you in their own time.

Gerry What?

Kate (*clapping her hands with delight*) Ha! Ha! I knew it! I think it's wonderful.

Julian Look, it was supposed to be a surprise and——

Gerry Surprise? It's certainly that! (*He heads for the telephone*)

Julian Please, Mrs Campbell. I should have kept my mouth shut.

Kate Don't worry, Julian. We won't let on it was you. Ha! Well done, Mary! Gerry, what are you doing?

Gerry (*dialling furiously*) What does it look like?

Kate You're not going to ring her.

Gerry Too damn right. I'm going to scotch this now before it gets out of hand.

Kate Gerry, you can't! You can't possibly discuss something as delicate as this on the phone!

Gerry Can't I?

Kate No!

Gerry You're right. There's no reply.

Kate They're probably at Roy's.

Gerry What d'you mean?

Kate What I say. They're probably at Roy's house.

Gerry At this time of night? She's usually in bed by... Oh, my God! Directory. What's his number?

Kate Gerry...

Gerry (*attacking the pages*) Bloody pages... Let's see—Winky, Winky...

Kate His name's Cartwright.

Gerry Course it is. Cartwright... Campion... Canford... Campbell! Here we are, this looks familiar: eight-three-nine-four.

Kate That's our number.

Gerry Damn it, so it is. Carson... Carter... Cartwright—here!

Kate Gerry——

Gerry Wing Commander, Wing Commander...

Kate You can't just ring him up. What will you say? "Excuse me, Wing Commander, but are you in bed——"

Gerry Don't! Don't even say it, Kate! Please!

Kate "Are you in bed with your teeth in?" is what I was actually——

Gerry OK! OK! I'll go round... (*He slams the phone down and grabs the army greatcoat*) What's this doing out? It belongs in the cupboard.

Gerry scrambles into the coat

Louise enters, all smiles

Louise Hi, Dad. Off out?

Gerry 'Fraid so. Bit of a flap on.

Louise (*yawning*) Well, I'm bushed. (*She kisses him*) Night, night.

Gerry Night, sweetheart. Sorry about all that stuff earlier. We'll discuss it in the morning.

Louise OK.

Gerry You too, Julian. I hope you'll be comfortable in my study.

Louise No, that's all right. He can sleep with me.

Gerry Good idea—*what*?

Louise Coming, Jay?

Gerry Hold it! That's far enough!

No-one moves

Louise Something wrong, Daddy?
Gerry You are not going to bed with this man.
Louise Yes, I am.
Gerry Not under my roof, you're not.
Louise I thought you wanted us to live together.
Gerry I do.
Louise Then, I'm rather confused.
Gerry Away from here, you can do what you like but in this house, under this roof—I will not have you bedding down with your boyfriend.
Louise Mmmh. An interesting conundrum. I'm a little too tired to tackle it now. As you say—we'll discuss it in the morning. Come on, Julian.
Gerry *(blocking the door)* Nope!
Louise Daddy—you're in Julian's way.
Gerry I'll stay here all night, if necessary.
Julian Actually, Mr Campbell—I do need the bathroom.
Gerry Huh. Nice try. You've only just been.
Louise Dad, will you stop being such a dick-head and let him through? *(To Kate)* Do something, will you? This is getting stupid.
Kate Gerry, if Julian needs to go to the loo, I think you'll have to let him.
Gerry No, I won't.
Kate I think you will.
Gerry He can go in the garden.
Kate Don't be so idiotic, Gerry and let Julian pass. *Gerry!*

Reluctantly, Gerry stands to one side

Julian belts across the room and up the stairs

Louise smiles triumphantly

Louise Sweet. He can hardly wait. Night.

Louise exits

Gerry stands pathetically in the greatcoat

Gerry This is mad. Crazy. What the hell's going on? What are you smiling at?

Kate You.

Gerry You find this amusing, do you?

Kate Hilarious. She's got you over a barrel, for once.

Gerry Really.

Kate 'Fraid so. It's your bed—you'll have to lie in it.

Gerry Oh, very droll. She's your daughter too, you know.

Kate Yes. I believe I can take some of the credit.

Gerry And you're quite content to permit this, are you?

Kate We don't have any choice, Gerry.

Gerry There's an ape in my daughter's bedroom!

Kate He's not an ape, he's your future son-in-law.

Gerry Oh, you think so.

Kate I'm certain of it. They're besotted. Louise is as stubborn as you are. I'm sure they'll be very happy.

Gerry This is preposterous. I can't stand here and do nothing.

Kate You can if you try. I wouldn't worry—she looks exhausted and he looks distinctly unwell. At worst, they'll curl up in each other's arms and sleep peacefully till morning.

Gerry I don't know what to say. I'm flabbergasted. My mother's up to God knows what with a pilot, my daughter's being deflowered under my very nose—and all you can come up with is a paragraph of Barbara Cartland.

Kate Oh, no. Barbara Cartland would have you and Julian with duvets at dawn on the terrace.

Gerry (*looking up to the ceiling*) What was that?

Kate What was what?

Gerry I heard a thump, a squeak—bed-spring or something.

Kate Don't be absurd.

Gerry There! Hear it?

Kate No!

Gerry God, I can't cope with this! I can't handle this at all!

Kate Well! At last we've heard it! Like the spring cuckoo after a long cold winter—Gerry says he "can't handle it".

Gerry Look. There's my daughter and my mother all in one evening. You're not being very sympathetic.

Kate No. I ran out of that some hours ago.

Gerry Then check the reserves. I may need it.

Kate Well, well—two of us standing at the window.

Gerry What?

Kate The rest of the world rushing purposefully by and there's two of us at the window.

Gerry I'm not in the mood for homilies.

Kate Are you going to stand there all night in that greatcoat?

Gerry I don't know.

Kate Come on, old soldier... (*She helps him off with it*) You've waged war on enough people for one day.

Gerry I feel—completely defeated.

Kate Oh, you are. You've been poisonous all evening and there isn't a single person you haven't insulted.

Gerry I must... I must do something.

Kate Like what? Rush up the road and deliver your mother from the jaws of depravity?

Gerry Oh, shut up.

Kate What, then?

Gerry I don't know! If I knew, I'd be doing it, wouldn't I?

Kate They don't need you, Gerry. You're not their saviour.

Gerry They're my flesh and blood.

Kate Don't you think you've enough to be getting on with? Here? With me? Gerry?

Gerry What?

Kate What are we going to do?

Gerry About what?

Kate Tomorrow. And the next day. And the next.

Gerry If tonight's anything to go by, I'll book a bed in intensive care.

Kate I want to know.

Gerry What d'you want me to say—I won't throw tantrums in restaurants anymore?

Kate I want you to say what you really think—what you *really* mean. Everyone else has had an earful this evening, why should I be left out? Come on. You've fiddled with their lives—how about mine? Mmmh?

Gerry I don't know, Kate! What is this—*In the Chair With Anthony Clare*? I don't know what I "really think", what I "really mean".

Kate No, I don't think you do. They're the first honest words you uttered all night. You say all these things about other people—you come out with all this stuff—but it's a blind, isn't it? You hold forth like a politician and switch positions like a Soho tart. And it's all rubbish. Your advice to those two, your concern for Mary—I don't believe a word of it. Not one word. And neither do you. But you can't help yourself—it comes out—you say it. Anything to distract you from what really matters. Because one brief glance in the mirror and you know you'll have to do something. You'll have to stop presuming the worst of the world and take your place with the rest of us—won't you?

Gerry "Physician heal thyself"—is that what you're trying to say?

Kate You're no physician. A phantom, more like.

Gerry So, you're going through a mid-life depression and it's all my fault.

Kate Oh, Gerry. It's not just you. It's not just me, either. It's neither of us. Instead of two people standing here, there's an empty space. Can't you sense that?

Gerry You really think so?

Kate Yes. I do.

Gerry That bad?

Kate We're right on the edge.

Gerry As far as I'm concerned—you're here, Kate. I know you're here. Oh, hell! The worst thing about conversations like this is it takes the spontaneity away. If I decide to buy you a bunch of flowers tomorrow——

Kate What?

Gerry Flowers. A bunch of flowers. If I decided to do that, it ceases to be a bunch of flowers—instead it's me "making an effort".

Kate This isn't about flowers, Gerry! I'm not talking about bloody flowers!

Gerry I know. I know that, but...

Kate Anyway, when was the last time you did that?

Gerry Not recently, I know, but——

Kate Quite.

Gerry Because you kept saying, "If only you'd buy me a bunch of flowers"! Immediately, it was spoiled. The one thing I couldn't do was buy you a bunch of stupid damn flowers! Look, do we have to go on with this? Marital navel-gazing wears me out.

Kate Yes, yes. Let's put it on ice. Stick it in the freezer with last summer's raspberries.

Gerry We've managed this far. We can muddle on a bit further.

Kate There you go again! You don't mean that. You can't seriously mean that, Gerry. Can you?

Gerry I don't know. I've so much on my mind...

Kate Well, it's not good enough! Our marriage is a habit. And what you're proposing is that we keep on doing it—until we can't, or won't, or drop dead! Well, I don't want that.

Gerry Habits aren't always bad.

Kate Yes, they are. They mean you're not thinking—only half alive.

Gerry So, what d'you want to do—kick it?

Kate Yes. Let's kick the habit.

Gerry Divorce, you mean.

Kate No! That's just defeat! By turning it into something else—something living. Let me ask you a question.

Gerry Oh God.

Kate If I could turn the clock back, would you do it again?

Gerry Where are we now—*Desert Island Discs*?

Kate Would you?

Gerry It's hypothetical. We can't wind the clock back—the time is now. It's go forwards or go under—backwards is not on offer.

Kate All right. The time is now, then, We're standing at the altar—all spruced up, the vicar's in his nightie, prayer book in hand——

Kate steers Gerry c, *facing out*

Gerry Kate...

Kate Prayer book in hand and questions at the ready. Now then.

Gerry You're being ridiculous.

Kate No, I'm not. (*She makes him kneel*) You're there, I'm next to you—all of a tremble, here in my veil (*She grabs Julian's shirt and puts it over her head*), "Do you Gerald Bartholomew take this Katherine Penelope——?"

Gerry Will you please stop this?

Kate "Katherine Penelope to be your wedded wife. To have and to hold for better or for worse... Something... Something, till death do you part, according to God's holy ordinances and thereto you plight her your troth?" Gerry? This is where you say "I do". This is where you plight me your troth. Gerry, will you please plight me your troth?

Gerry You're being very childish.

Kate Am I?

Gerry Yes. And you've got it all wrong. You don't plight your troth and then say "I do", you say "I will" and then you plight troths.

Kate Really?

Gerry Yes. The troth plighting comes later—after the ring.

Kate I didn't know you were such an expert. You've obviously done it before.

Gerry Oh, for God's sake.

Louise appears in the doorway and observes them. She has her dressing-gown and glasses on, her hair tied back and looks strangely like a child again

Louise You know, it's extraordinary but every time I enter this room it gets progressively more bizarre.
Kate (*to Louise*) Did you want something, angel?
Louise Kaolin and Morphine—have we got some?
Kate Yes. Is someone unwell?
Louise Julian. He's thrown up twice.
Gerry Oh dear. Poor chap.
Kate I'll just get it. It's in the kitchen. Hold this a minute, will you?

Kate exits giving the shirt to Louise

Brief pause

Louise The steak, probably.
Gerry Possibly.
Louise Dad?
Gerry Mmmh?
Louise I know I'm going to regret this but... Why did Mum have Julian's shirt on her head just now?
Gerry Julian's shirt?
Louise Yes... No! Whosever. What was she doing?
Gerry Nothing much. Just getting married.
Louise Ah. Right. That explains it. Who to? Anyone I know?
Gerry Me. That's all.
Louise Fine. Just wondered, you know.

Kate enters

Kate Here we are. This should sort him out.
Louise Thanks... Don't forget your veil.
Kate Sorry? Oh, right. Thank you.
Louise Night.
Gerry Night, sweetheart.
Kate Night, darling.

Louise turns at the door and crosses back to Gerry. She kisses him on both cheeks

Louise You may be a pig but at least you care. I'll always love you for that... (*About to go, she turns and puts their hands together*) I hope you'll both be very happy.

She exits

Kate and Gerry stand for a brief second with hands clasped, then break

Gerry I really am very tired.
Kate Me too.

Kate starts turning out lights individually and plumping cushions, etc. Gerry picks up the phone

Kate What are you doing?
Gerry Trying Mother again. See if she's back.

Kate opens the curtains aggressively, Gerry changes his mind and replaces the receiver. As Kate passes him to turn out the last light, he takes her gently by the shoulders. She won't look at him. He lifts her chin and kisses her tenderly on the mouth

I'm sorry.

She puts her arms around him. They hold each other

Kate Come on. We're both tired.
Gerry Wait.
Kate Please, Gerry—I'm done in.
Gerry Will you marry me?
Kate Don't be silly.

She tries to pull away. He doesn't let go. She holds her wedding finger up to his face

What d'you think this is—a diamond studded growth?
Gerry Yes or no.

She looks away. He lifts her chin again

Kate I'm not sure.

Gerry What?

Kate Well... I've only known you about twenty three years—I need time to think. You're not after my money, are you?

Gerry No. Just your body.

Kate Oh, very funny.

Gerry Just your hand—to hold in the dark.

Kate Two old people keeping each other company?

Gerry No, one old person being nursed by a gorgeous youth.

Kate Flatterer. You don't need nursing.

Gerry smiles. Brief pause. Then he looks at her, horrified

Gerry I'm the youth!

She pushes him back onto the sofa

Kate Is that so? (*She climbs onto him*) Let's see what you're made of then, shall we?

Gerry Ow! Get off me!

She pulls open his shirt

What are you doing?

Kate Checking the merchandise... Oh, Gerry! Look at you! Just look at you!

Gerry What is it! What's wrong?

Kate And I thought I had saggy boobs! You're fat, you're old, you're difficult... But I love you—so, so much. (*She kisses him passionately*) Pompous old fart!

They kiss again. Kate reaches across and switches out the remaining lamp. In the half-light she nestles in beside him on the sofa

Gerry Now, what are you doing?

Kate Remember the old days?

Gerry Kate, we can't... Ow! They'll hear us upstairs.

Kate Come on, fatso—budge up.

Gerry No, really, I can't. I've got the most terrible headache.

Kate ignores him and pulls the greatcoat over their heads. With attendant giggling, they squeeze up together. Brief pause. A torch light outside shines through the window. The beam scans the room and then vanishes

Louise enters. As she crosses the room in the half-light she registers Julian's shirt draped over the back of the sofa and then moving lumps under the greatcoat below. She retrieves the shirt and tip-toes the rest of the way into the kitchen, shutting the door

Kate pops her head out from under the coat

Kate What was that? Did you hear something?
Gerry (*also popping his head out*) Don't think so.

The sound of the front door opening and whispered voices in the hall. Kate and Gerry dive under the greatcoat again

Mary and Roy enter from the hall shining a torch

Mary (*whispering*) Yes. They are—they're in bed.
Roy (*whispering*) Where d'you think you left them?
Mary (*whispering*) On the side. I'm sure they must be on the side.
Roy (*loudly*) D'you think it would help if——
Mary Ssshhhh!
Roy (*whispering*) D'you think it would help if we whistled?
Mary (*whispering*) Yes, all right. But for heaven's sake, do it quietly.

They both attempt a low whistle. In the dark, Roy steps back into the armchair. In trying to steady himself, he takes Mary with him

Roy Ow! Damn and blast!
Mary What are you doing, Roy? Mind!

The light shines from the kitchen as Louise enters. She hurries across the room to switch on the main lights by the door

Roy and Mary flail about in the armchair

Louise I don't believe this.
Mary Oh Wheezy, darling. Such a stupid thing—I've locked myself out. Left my keys here somewhere.

Roy I offered to put her up at my place but she wouldn't have it.
Mary Not until your spare room's ready.
Roy You could have had my bed. I'd have kipped on the sofa.
Mary Don't be absurd. With your rheumatism, you'd have woken up stuck. I'd have had to get the fire brigade or something. Now, come on—let's find these keys.

Louise helps them both out of the chair and they begin searching

Louise Whereabouts did you leave them?
Mary I'm not sure. Whistle, or clap, or something.

They all begin whistling and clapping round the room

Julian appears in the doorway in boxer shorts. He stands and observes the strange ritual

Julian What's going on?
Louise Trying to find Granny's keys. Don't just stand there—help!

Julian joins in

Mary It sometimes works better if you "la".

They follow Mary la-la-ing round the room. Suddenly a bleep is heard. They sing again. The bleep replies. Step by step they all converge on the sofa. Mary pulls back the greatcoat to reveal a bare-chested Gerry and a dishevelled Kate

There they are!

Mary plunges her hand into the sofa and pulls out the keys. She plants a kiss on Kate's and Gerry's heads

Sorry to have disturbed you both. Now, come along, Roy. And you, Wheezy—I don't want those two putting ideas into your heads. Or yours, Roy. (*She moves to the exit*) We'll see ourselves out! You two get to bed!
Roy Night, all!

Mary and Roy exit

Julian follows—lingering slightly to take in Kate and Gerry on the sofa. Louise pushes him out of the room with a "don't stare" look

She turns at the door. Kate and Gerry pull the greatcoat up to their chins like guilty children

Louise D'you want the lights on or off? I'll switch them off, shall I? At your age you're better off in the dark.

Louise switches out the light

Black-out

CURTAIN

FURNITURE AND PROPERTY LIST

Further dressing may be added at the director's discretion

ACT I

On stage: Small dining table
Dining chairs
Table lamps
Sofa. *On it:* cushions
Armchair
Cupboards. *In them:* large army greatcoat, cleaner's housecoat
Telephone directory
Yellow Pages
TV set
Telephone
Bunch of house keys
Blow-heater
Small framed photo
Poker
Bottle of gin
Glasses
Mirror
Vase. *In it:* dried flowers

Off stage: Huge pot plant (**Julian**)
Tea tray (**Mary**)
Sock (**Gerry**)
Carrier bag. *In it:* shopping (**Gerry**)
Golf clubs (**Roy**)
Bottle of champagne, box of glasses (**Julian**)
Walking sticks (**Mary**)
2 raw steaks (**Gerry**)
Meat hammer (**Gerry**)

Personal: **Kate:** wedding ring, car keys
Louise: spectacles
Roy: spectacles, handkerchief
Mary: bag, keys, handkerchief, wine gums

ACT II

On stage:	As before
Set:	Army greatcoat **Mary's** keys
Strike:	Bunch of house keys
Off stage:	Box. *In it:* glasses, keys (**Roy**) Tea towel (**Gerry**) Tray. *On it:* pair of plates with steaks, cutlery (**Gerry**)

LIGHTING PLOT

Property fittings required: table lamps, wall lights. Practical fittings required: table lamp
Interior. The same scene throughout

ACT I ˙Evening

To open: Small table lamp on

Cue 1	**Louise**: "…stop asking questions and——" *Bring up passing car headlight effect*	(Page 3)
Cue 2	**Louise** flicks on the lights *Bring up general lighting*	(Page 4)
Cue 3	**Gerry** switches TV set on *Bring up flicker of TV*	(Page 8)
Cue 4	**Gerry** switches the lights off *Fade lights*	(Page 9)
Cue 5	**Kate** switches the TV off, lights back on *Snap off TV, bring up general lighting*	(Page 9)
Cue 6	**Gerry** exits switching off the lights *Fade lights*	(Page 10)
Cue 7	**Kate** switches the lights back on *Bring up general lighting*	(Page 10)
Cue 8	**Louise** begins turning the lights out *Fade lights slightly*	(Page 25)
Cue 9	**Louise** switches out the lights *Fade lights*	(Page 25)

Close to the Wind   69

Cue 10   After we hear a car pulling away   (Page 25)
             Bring up kitchen light

Cue 11   **Kate** switches on the lights.   (Page 26)
             Bring up general lighting

Cue 12   **Gerry** enters from the kitchen   (Page 35)
             Black-out

ACT II   Evening

To open: General overall lighting

Cue 13   **Kate** starts turning out lights individually   (Page 61)
             Fade lights as appropriate

Cue 14   **Kate** switches out the remaining lamp   (Page 62)
             Fade lights

Cue 15   Shortly after **Kate** and **Gerry** squeeze up together (Page 63)
             Bring up torch light effect from outside

Cue 16   **Louise** enters   (Page 63)
             Bring up kitchen light

Cue 17   **Louise** turns on the main lights by the door   (Page 63)
             Bring up general lighting

Cue 18   **Louise** switches out the light   (Page 65)
             Black-out

Cue 19   At end of Act II   (Page 65)
             Black-out

EFFECTS PLOT

ACT I

Cue 1   **Julian** and **Louise** watch and listen   (Page 3)
Car doors slam

Cue 2   **Julian:** "It's a bloody cupboard!"   (Page 3)
Front door slams

Cue 3   **Gerry** turns TV set on   (Page 8)
Documentary drones on

Cue 4   As **Kate** looks at TV   (Page 9)
TV programme as script page 9

Cue 5   **Gerry** moves out of sight   (Page 9)
Front door slams

Cue 6   **Julian:** "Think so."   (Page 10)
Sound of keys in front door

Cue 7   **Kate** switches the lights back on   (Page 10)
Car horn sounds impatiently

Cue 8   **Kate** hurries out   (Page 10)
Car door slams, car starts up and pulls away

Cue 9   Shortly after the kitchen door shuts   (Page 16)
Front door opens and slams shut

Cue 10   **Roy** continues studying the small picture   (Page 17)
Front door opens

Cue 11   **Louise** and **Julian** scamper past the windows   (Page 17)
Front door slams shut

Cue 12   **Roy:** "Zap!"   (Page 22)
Bleep

Cue 13   **Louise** switches out the lights and they exit   (Page 25)
            Front door slams shut, car doors slam, car pulls away

Cue 14   **Kate**: "Are you up here?"   (Page 26)
            Car pulls up, car door slams, keys in the front door

Cue 15   **Kate** enters   (Page 26)
            Banging in the kitchen

Cue 16   **Kate**: "Get off me, Gerry! Please!"   (Page 34)
            Front door slams shut

ACT II

Cue 17   **Gerry** whistles   (Page 36)
            Bleep

Cue 18   **Louise** exits into the hall   (Page 48)
            Front door slams shut

Cue 19   **Gerry**: "Don't think so."   (Page 63)
            Front door opens

Cue 20   They all "la-la" round the room   (Page 64)
            Bleeps as appropriate

PRINTED IN GREAT BRITAIN BY
THE LONGDUNN PRESS LTD., BRISTOL.